JADE

玉

Text and Photographs
Fred Ward

Editing
Charlotte Ward

When ideal color and clarity combine, Burma's jadeite appears true green, a hue so intense with a translucency so glowing that the gem is often confused with emerald. Such rare specimens, the jade world's most expensive, enjoy a special name, "imperial jade." This spectacular example, owned by the government of Burma (now called Myanmar), is in Rangoon.

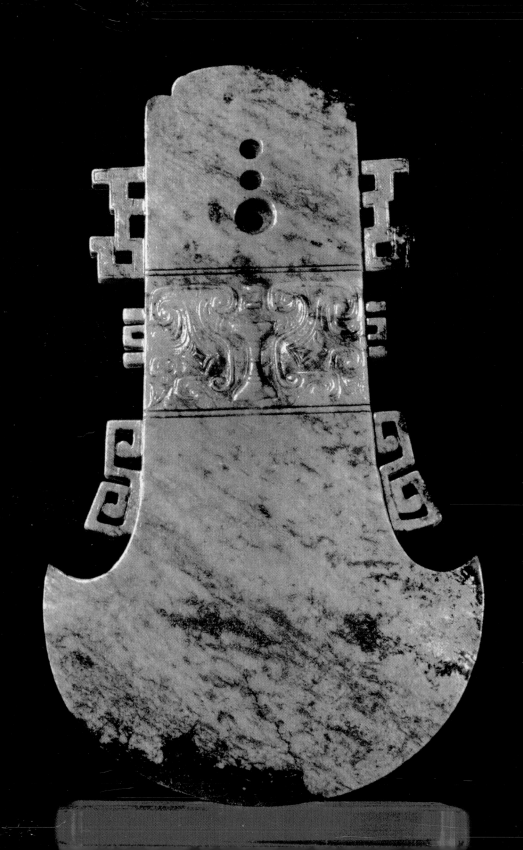

In the
Beginning

Jade—say the magic word. Whisper it. *Jade*. Let its sound transport you to dreams of the Orient, to soft nights. Can you see a shadowed inn high in an isolated rain forest? Royal guests arriving by elephant? A luscious dinner served on pure white stone? *Jade*. A couple walking down a long pebbled beach. The color of a wide tropical leaf backlit by the morning sun. *Jade*. A green so rich and pure that it brings spring into your heart. *Jade*. Dream your dream.

The exotic visions jade evokes are real, true, and deserved. To the Chinese for thousands of years, jade was the *Stone of Heaven*. As you shall see, they treasured jade beyond any other material. Europeans and Americans might desire diamonds or gold, but they do not revere either. The Chinese centered their culture around jade, exhibiting an impassioned love as old as China itself, one that transcended our present understanding.

But the story of jade is even more complex than that single historic relationship; for jade is global, its use ancient, and its position as a bridge between gems and minerals unique. Someone, somewhere, lost in the mists of time, realized that jade made a better tool than anything else ever had. We now know that momentous discovery occurred more than 5,000 years ago, reflecting an instant of genius independently repeated in a variety of future locations around the world.

Today's industrialized societies can choose what will make the most effective tools, weapons, and art from a host of metals, plastics, glass, minerals, and other materials. Imagine living in prehistoric times when the choices were limited to rocks, wood, crystals, and other naturally occurring objects. Metals had not yet been worked when people first began using jade. Although it was a stone, because of its characteristics, jade conferred many of the benefits of metal. Even after humans moved into the Iron and Bronze Ages, their Stone Age jade tools performed better than early metals, a situation that existed until we recently perfected especially hard steels.

Symbolism and beauty coincide in China's ancient ceremonial nephrite jade carvings. This complex **ch'i**, *or ax head, from the Warring States period (476-221 B.C.) illustrates the Chinese devotion to jade.*

The National Museum, Singapore

3

Having access to stones harder and tougher than the neighbors' produced distinct advantages. It is no surprise that the oldest jade artifacts were practical. Wherever jade occurred, early humans recognized its potential, fashioned it into tools and weapons, then ritualized its use by making symbolic pieces that usually reflected its initial utilitarian shapes. In a society and culture as old as China's, honoring any specific gem, metal, or stone for millennia resulted in a trove of utensils, symbolic artifacts, and art, as well as myths and legends.

In a similar time period half a world apart, European peoples capitalized on jade's special qualities. Around Lake Konstanz, in what is now Switzerland, a "stilt-house culture" developed on the edges of several local lakes. Between 3500 and 1800 B.C., a small Alpine group gathered pieces of both jadeite and nephrite—the two materials we know today as jade—mainly to fashion them into axes and adzes. The British Museum once printed a survey of prehistoric jade ax discoveries in Europe, documenting hundreds of jadeite and nephrite examples in the British Isles, France, Germany, Switzerland, Italy, and Yugoslavia.

Chinese burial sites dated from about the same period include nephrite artifacts with important differences. Whereas the Swiss stilt-house cultures apparently never progressed to ritualizing jade, even the oldest Chinese relics include symbolic jade carvings. However early the Chinese formed jade tools, they apparently immediately began to honor the material by also carving it into their most precious possessions.

4

Symbolic and practical—a pi *disc (opposite), the most revered of six ritual jade forms the Chinese believed bridged earthly existence to immortality. Sui Dynasty signets (above) authenticated messages between emperor and generals. And Swiss tribes in 3000 B.C. used nephrite hatchet blades to chop wood and kill prey.*

B y now you have noticed that two different names, *nephrite* and *jadeite*, apply to jade. Through the resulting confusion, unscrupulous sellers take advantage of baffled buyers. In gemology, only with jade does one word describe two chemically different rocks. I deliberately use the word *rock* instead of *mineral* to classify jade. Rocks, such as both jades as well as lapis lazuli, alabaster, and jasper, are aggregates of one or more minerals. A mineral has a definite chemical composition and characteristic structure with consistent physical and optical properties. A mineral is the component; a rock is a collection of minerals. Although nephrite and jadeite are both green and both hard, they are no more the same than emerald and tourmaline or chrysoprase and peridot. Further complicating our saga is the realization that China's most honored stone—the creamy white jade reserved for royal carvings—was nephrite, whereas today, the only jade considered gem-quality is jadeite, which fetches ever-soaring prices.

Historic accidents are largely responsible for applying one term to two different stones. By the time Spain conquered the New World, even though Europeans had shown a penchant for labeling all natural things, they had not yet classified the rocks so esteemed by the Chinese and vital to the Swiss stilt-house cultures. Within a few years after Columbus set sail, Spanish *conquistadores* adopted the Mesoamerican Indian custom of wearing local bright green rocks around the waist or in pockets to cure kidney disorders. Their name for the kidney cure, *piedra de ijada*—stone of the loins, stuck, and was transported back to Europe, where jade's reputation spread to other countries. In France the phrase should have translated literally *pierre de l'ejade*, but in what may have been a printer's error, it appeared as *le jade*.

The Renaissance brought a scientific revolution to Europe and with it, Latin taxonomy. The Mesoamerican green rock, by then called *piedra de los riñones*—stone of the kidneys—became *lapis nephriticus*, which translated to English as *nephrite*. So for a couple of centuries the word *nephrite* was used for the material we now know as *jadeite*.

As a result of early English, Spanish, and Portuguese trade, Chinese jade was well known in Europe. In 1863, French scientist Alexis Damour

Auckland Museum, New Zealand

After tools and utensils, jade cultures used their most treasured material for symbols and decorations. Poised as if to speak, an animated figure tops the 758 A.D. Mayan portrait jar from Tikal (left).

New Zealand's Maoris carved Marakihau (above), nephrite sea monsters.

The only known example of a Mayan portrait head fashioned from a single jadeite stone (opposite) was part of a royal belt assembly. From the Maya Classic Period (600-800 A.D), the carving was unearthed in Honduras.

National Museum of Anthropology, Guatemala

noticed that some of the bright green jewelry and carvings arriving from Burma looked very different from ancient Chinese carvings. Using new analytical tools, Damour observed two distinct chemical compositions. He applied the already accepted word *nephrite* to old Chinese jades and created a new name, *jadeite*, for the Burmese material. As if that were not confusing enough, later analysis revealed that Mesoamerican jade, for which the word *nephrite* had been created, has the same chemistry as Burma's jadeite. Even though China never associated kidneys with jade, it was left with the Latin kidney connection. Unable to correct the linguistic and mineralogical tangle, scientists let both names and definitions stand, and the world has two jades.

Nephrite, China's historic jade, is a silicate of calcium and magnesium, part of the amphibole group, which ranges from pure white (actinolite, absent of iron) to green (tremolite, colored by iron). In addition to chemistry, nephrite is defined by physical structure; it must have felted interlocking fibers, which give nephrite its unique resistance to breaking, thus making it the "toughest" natural material (see page 21). Nephrite occurs in British Columbia (the largest commercial producer), Australia, New Zealand, Russia, South Korea, Taiwan, Poland, Taiwan, South Africa, California, Alaska, Wyoming, Nevada, and in small deposits in far western China. There, local jade pickers walk the White Jade and Black Jade Rivers, looking for rare white pebbles, cobbles, and boulders, once prized by Chinese emperors. But nature doles out only a few hundred a year, keeping white nephrite one of the rarest materials of all time.

The British Museum, London

Jadeite, a silicate of sodium and aluminum, was the Maya's most precious possession. Chromium causes its vibrant green color, prized by Chinese royalty and today's buyers. Jadeite is mined in Burma, Guatemala, and Russia, with small deposits located in Japan, Switzerland, and California.

A timeline helps to tell the story of both nephrite and jadeite. Artifacts show that the Chinese reverence for nephrite was fully developed at least 5,000 years ago. They traded for jade from a deposit in the western Kunlun Mountains to produce the finest stone carvings the world has ever seen. Later, Europeans made tools from both nephrite and jadeite between 3500 and 1800 B.C. Simultaneously, prehistoric inhabitants of Swiss stilt-houses made axes from both nephrite and jadeite between 3500 and 1800 B.C. Between 1500 B.C. and 400 A.D., the Olmec in Mesoamerica worked a jadeite deposit that served three cultures for 3,000 years. Following the Olmec, the Maya added significantly to jade art by carving their most precious religious and symbolic objects in jadeite until about 900 A.D. Then came the Aztecs, who treasured jadeite until they were overrun by the Spanish in the 1500s. Across the Pacific, the Maori arrived in New Zealand around 1000 A.D., discovered nephrite, and centered their life around the material up to the 1800s. Only in the late 1700s did Burma introduce its jadeite to the world.

CHINA AND THE STONE OF HEAVEN

When people were new on the earth and prey to all the wild animals, the Storm God looked down from the heavens and took pity. With one hand he grasped the rainbow and with the other forged it into jade axes. These he threw down for people to find. And so they did, and once discovering the axes, guessed the origin of their precious gift, and thereafter called jade *the stone of heaven.*

A Chinese Legend

If jade is discarded and pearls destroyed, petty thieves will disappear, there being no valuables left to steal.

Dictionary from reign of
Emperor K'ang Hsi (A.D. 1662-1722)

Tradition has it that Confucius, China's best-known intellectual, was born after a unicorn delivered a jade tablet to his mother. The birth announcement bore an inscription calling the boy "a throneless king." Such was the Chinese regard for the perfection of this stone that at times, where we apply *gold* or *silver* as superlatives—such as "golden-toned," "streets paved with gold," or "silver-tongued"—the Chinese prefix *jade*, especially when referring to women. They call a beautiful woman "jade person"; a woman's smooth skin "fragrant jade"; her hands "jade bamboo shoots"; her especially sweet singing voice "jade rich"; and the death of one possessing those attributes "jade shattered." Poetically *jade* describes many other aspects of life. Gazing at a full moon, the Chinese admire a "jade plate"; when only a crescent remains, they cast their eyes toward a "jade hook" and toast it with wine cradled in a "jade boat."

Richard Gump, who started buying and collecting jade in China early in the twentieth century, said, "China built a civilization around the stone." As Gump became famous for his San Francisco store, he wrote, "...the use of jade is inseparably linked with the development of Chinese worship, court ceremonials, thought, and art..." I know of no historical parallel. Even though the Spanish pillaged the New World, decimating indigenous cultures

As one of the six Chinese ritual jade forms, the ts'ung, *a tube of nephrite, symbolizes Earth. This richly-hued example dates from the Western Zhou period, eleventh century to 770 B.C.*

Honolulu Academy of Arts, Hawaii

9

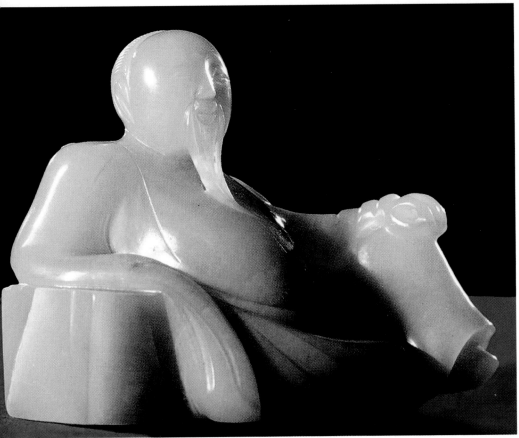

in their crazed search for treasure, they never made gold and silver their *raison d'être*, their reason for being. The Chinese saying goes, "One can put a price on gold, but jade is priceless."

To the Chinese, jade transcended value, rarity, beauty, and lust. Only through jade in a disc-shaped *pi* (pronounced "bee") could emperors speak directly to even greater powers, thus completing the cosmic link between Heaven and Earth. No culture has ever assigned such a role to any other material.

At the highest levels of Chinese society jade played an integral part in everyday life. The first objects the emperor touched each morning were jade—most often white nephrite. Scholars were allowed to have their writing implements of jade. Respect for the stone was such that after Emperor Qian Long, who displayed perhaps the greatest devotion to jade, assembled the empire's best craftsmen in his Beijing workshops, he decreed that jade masters henceforth were to be referred to as "Sir," a distinct honor in the caste-conscious culture.

Gentlemen paced their lives by adjusting their gait so the jade pieces dangling from their belts tinkled a measured beat. Confucius, whose writings both reflected and established the essence of Chinese life, listed among these requisite jadelike characteristics gentlemen should aspire to: virtue, loyalty,

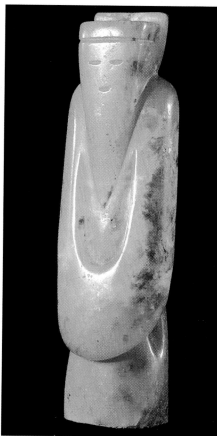

Age and nephrite were naturally associated and equally revered. White exemplified scholarship, wisdom, and maturity, so white jade perfectly suited figurines of two elderly scholars. Elegantly simple lines completed with reserve characterize an aristocrat pendant (right) from the Han Dynasty (206 B.C.-220 A.D.). By the Qing Dynasty (1644-1912), human details were considerably more complicated (left). Painstaking work on jade, a hard, tough material, often took months or years, even with a treadle (above).

intelligence, justice, humanity, and truth. In the master's time, after contests of skill, third place received an ivory scepter; second place won gold; only the first place winner commanded jade.

Many fanciful stories but few firm facts enlighten us about the origins of jade and jade carving. As is the case with Egypt and other great archeological sites, scientists often collect the finest artifacts from the protective environment of tombs. Fortunately, Chinese culture expressed itself in nephrite, a material that does not rot or age, one that preserves history almost perfectly. Even though jade cannot be dated, burial relics can. Ritual jades almost as old as jade utensils indicate that the stone's earliest users, working more than 5,000 years ago, honored nephrite's special qualities of beauty, hardness, and toughness.

Despite claims to the contrary, there appears to be no historical source for jade within China's traditional borders. The millions of carvings over thousands of years all seem to have been shaped from imported Kunlun Mountains nephrite. The Chinese have always gotten jade from the same source. As a result of border expansion after World War II, those mountains now lie within China's borders instead of in Turkestan (see Chapter 5).

One of the stops on the famed Silk Road, Hotan (formerly spelled

11

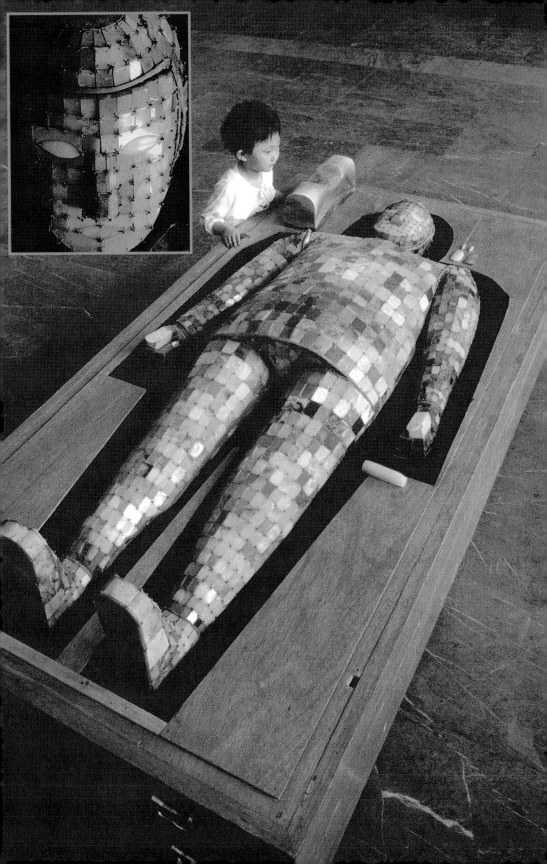

Khotan) facilitated trade between Europe and Asia long before ocean commerce existed. At the edge of the great Taklimakan Desert near the confluence of the White Jade River (Yurungkax) and Black Jade River (Karakax), Hotan served as trading center, way-station, and site of the first Asian nephrite sighting by a European.

Marco Polo, the intrepid Italian adventurer, traveler, and writer, watched small boulders being lifted by hand from the area's two rivers and transported by caravan to Beijing, where they "fetched great prices." Unfortunately, neither he nor any other European in 1272 knew enough about gems and minerals to identify the rocks properly as nephrite, which explains why he noted, in error, large numbers of "chalcedonies and jaspers." What Polo witnessed was the time-honored jade collection process, little changed in the four thousand years before he arrived or in the intervening seven hundred years before I waded into those same waters to pluck out a few precious pebbles of my own.

No "jade mine" exists in the Kunlun mountains above Hotan. Uygur tribesmen and the Chinese government try from time to time to mine *in situ* deposits by either heating or freezing boulders to coerce cracking. Where they have had little success, nature's seasons mine steadily, slowly feeding man's greed. Winter's expansion, contraction, and melting wash jade pebbles and boulders from cliffs and river banks into raging spring rivers, which tumble them downstream toward Hotan. Along the way Uygur "jade pickers" walk along the banks, or in the water when possible, looking for jade. A skilled picker with a donkey or a strong back can still make more money from jade in one or two months than from farming all year.

Far better than reality is the Chinese jade collection myth. A long time ago, so the story goes, the local custom was to have young maidens strip and walk naked in the rivers at night. Because the unclothed females (*yin*) would naturally attract the male (*yang*) jade, they had only to feel the nephrite pebbles rubbing against their feet to reach down and pick them up.

We know the earliest Chinese found and honored nephrite, among the hardest substances and certainly the toughest available to them. Because it neither chipped nor flaked but kept a good edge, it made fine tools and weapons. But the most ancient examples are too small, too thin, and too delicately carved to have been practical. As meticulous as the Chinese were in keeping records and calendars, it seems the strangest of oversights that they omitted the origin of their use of jade, their most precious possession. The oldest records in China's vast written history include stories of nephrite jade carving and the special reverence and esteem with which it was held. I conjecture that the Chinese may have recut their tools and weapons into ceremonial and ritual symbols or that jade use predates writing, hence the Chinese have no record or cultural memory of a time without jade.

A suit fit for a king. Reserved for royalty, jade burial suits were coincidentally used in China and Mexico. Only emperors merited gold wire to connect more than 2000 mosaic jade tiles. Lesser rulers, such as King Liu Yen, who died in 90 A.D., made do with less noble metals (left).

Hebei Provincial Museum, Shijiazhuang, China

Animal Magic

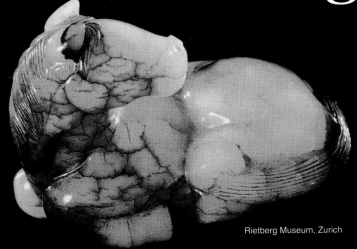

Chinese artists have displayed their understanding of animals with deeply sensitive carvings. A Ming Dynasty (1368-1644 A.D) horse (above) has smiled through centuries while a similar Song Dynasty horse (right) continues to slumber peacefully. Representing a cosmic force capable of great good, a large, respectfully carved dragon pendant (below from the Western Zhou period, dates from 1027 B.C. to 770 B.C.

Many Chinese carvings represent fantasies. A winged unicorn (above) from the eighteenth century Qing Dynasty (1644-1911 A.D.) appears to have just alighted. Another winged beast, a pi-hsieh (left), still stands guard from the Ming Dynasty. An imaginary "strange beast" (below), carved in the Song Dynasty (960-1279 A.D.), seems to be materializing from a white nephrite cobble.

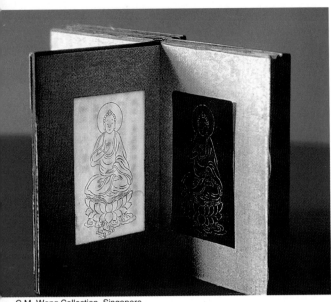

Intricacy almost beyond comprehension characterizes a collection of Buddhist sutras in a Qing Dynasty prayer book created for an empress. Gold-leaf-filled characters are carved into both sides of eighth-inch thin nephrite sheets with such precision that the back-to-back writing is invisible on the opposite side. The complex design makes it possible to read the sutras either by light reflected from the gold leaf or transmitted through the thin jade pages.

C.M. Wong Collection, Singapore

The First Carver

Before Earth's creation, there was a great Void, in which was created Chaos, which in time separated into Dark (Yin, which was female and represented Earth) and Light (Yang, which was male and represented the Sun). In time the two met and merged. From their union Pan Ku, a dwarf, was formed. With his hands, a hammer, and a chisel Pan Ku set about carving the universe from Chaos. Four supernatural beings appeared to help this First Carver: the Unicorn, the Tortoise, the Phoenix, and the Dragon. Significantly, the last two were seen as the essence of Yang, the male, and they were composed of white and azure blue jade. Each day Pan Ku toiled, he grew in proportion to his accomplishments. And he carved for 18,000 years. When he died he was so large and so integrated with his task that he became part of his creation. Pan Ku's flesh became Earth's soil, his head its mountains. His veins formed its rivers, his skin plants, his hair trees, his teeth and bones became its minerals, his marrow its precious gems. His right eye lit the sun, his left the moon. His last breath became thunder, clouds, and wind, his sweat fell as rain. And from the creatures that fed on his body came Man.

Taoist Legend

No matter where they lived, the world's peoples have cycled through similar eras: the eolithic, when they used bones or flint chips as tools; the paleolithic, when people chipped stones to form knives and ax heads; the neolithic or Stone Age, characterized by polished stone tools; then usually the Bronze and Iron Ages. The Maori in New Zealand and the Maya in Mesoamerica left jade tools older than their ritual jade carvings. Unlike those jade cultures, I have yet to see any eolithic or paleolithic jades from China. Even their earliest tools, displayed in collections and museums, had been polished and often elaborately and beautifully decorated, suggesting ritual use. Because the Chinese capitalized on nephrite's metal-like characteristics,

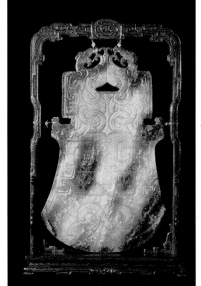

Reserved for royalty and the elite, white nephrite, the most valuable material throughout Chinese history, brings life to two great carvings. The **kuang,** *a Song Dynasty (960-1279 A.D.) drinking horn, displays a hornless dragon motif, and the Warring States ax head may be the best* **ch'i** *ever carved.*

they may have bypassed or substantially shortened their Stone Age. No wonder they exalted jade.

Nephrite jade's position in Chinese religious services, ceremonies, burials, and mythology is unprecedented. From their legends it is clear they believed jade and people were intertwined from the beginning. For nearly four millennia of organized imperial court religious rites, which centered on obedience to heaven, jade played the pivotal role. Six objects in particular were of supreme importance in both religious rites and burials.

Of all jade forms, the *pi* was most significant (see page 4). In burials, it was placed under the deceased's back. *Pi* was both the symbol for heaven and the emperor's conduit when he wished to speak to heaven. *Pi* forms can be undecorated or filled with small, raised circles. Ideally, the hole in the middle should be a fifth the diameter of the entire flat jade disk, which makes each jade side twice as wide as the hole. The origin of the *pi* form becomes clear when you compare it to the Chinese symbol for the sun, ☉.

Second, the *ts'ung*, is a yellow nephrite cylinder with four flat sides or prisms (see page 8), which may have had dual meaning: the four Chinese elements—fire, water, wood, and metal—or the cardinal compass points—North, East, South, and West. A fifth element, Earth, was represented by the *ts'ung* itself. In burials, it often rested on the deceased's abdomen or chest, thus placing the dead between Heaven (*pi*) and Earth (*ts'ung*). Scholars have often attributed sexual symbolism to *ts'ung*, but Westerners find such a relationship less than obvious. By the Han Dynasty (206 B.C.-220 A.D.) use

17

White Is Beautiful

Carved from white nephrite found in the Kunlun mountains south of Hotan in what is now China, this royal wine cup (above), with flower base and wild goat's head handle, was made for Indian ruler Shah Jehan, who built the Taj Mahal. To flex their creative muscles and demonstrate their carving skills, artists in the Ming Dynasty made white nephrite flower buttons from single pebbles, which had to be resewn onto clothes for every wearing. A square knot in jade from the Qing Dynasty testifies to the anonymous artist's skill and patience.

Like a general's shoulder stars, nephrite **kuei** *tablets (right) signified rank in ancient China. Some were unadorned, but this Zhou Dynasty example incorporates a grain pattern. Just as some Chinese today use stone name stamps, called* **chops,** *emperors once sealed official decrees with jade signatures. Emperor Guangxii, who assumed power in 1875, used this white nephrite seal, (right) whose handle includes a double-headed dragon. Carved in China during the Qing Dynasty from white Burma jadeite using India's Mogul style, a teapot of unsurpassed delicacy illustrates utility soaring to the highest expression of artistry. Rubies, red spinels, and precise surface details*   *complete the decoration of this*   *breathtakingly thin translucent*   *treasure.*

Kuei; C.M. Wong Collection

Seal; Lizzadro Museum of Lapidary Art, Elmhurst, Illinois

The Baur Collection, Geneva

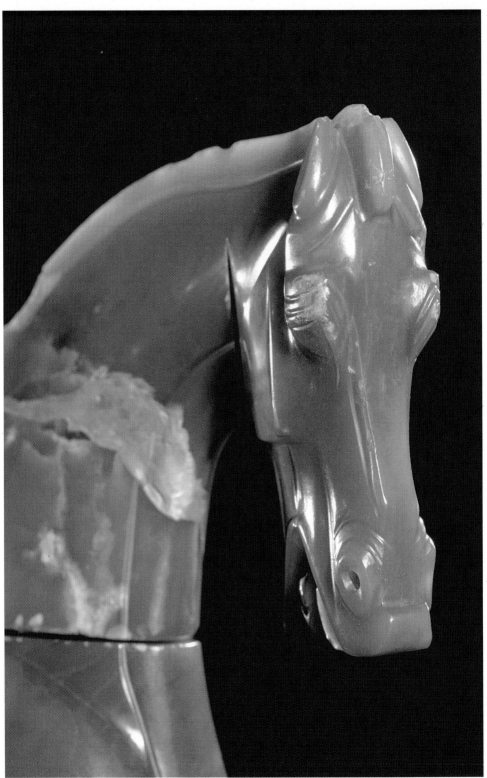

National Palace Museum, Taipei

Nephrite thin-section photomicrograph, 200x

Jadeite thin-section photomicrograph, 100x

Chemical as well as cultural differences distinguish nephrite from jadeite. Fluid lines and an artist's appreciation for the creature's internal being define a Six Dynasties (265-581 A.D.) nephrite masterpiece as perhaps the greatest horse carving in history (opposite). In comparison, a Qing Dynasty multicolored jadeite horse exhibits flash, but no soul. Nephrite's toughness and subtle character result from its felted, fibrous composition (above, left). Jadeite's interlocked crystalline structure and its chemistry (above, right) produce intense colors and glassy finishes.

of the *ts'ung* as an Earth symbol was common. Older *ts'ung* are sometimes two or more feet high, whereas later examples tend to be shorter. Carvers will note that the *pi* is a relatively simple form, easy to make with primitive tools even when decorated with a raised circular grain pattern. But the more complicated *ts'ung* requires additional skill and probably metal tools and harder abrasives. As they improved their tools, the Chinese also improved their carving technique.

The third ritual jade form, the *kuei*, was often carved in blue-green nephrite. Its pointed flat stylized shape probably derived from swords or knives (see page 19). The Chinese placed this symbol of imperial power, Spring, and the East to the left of corpses.

21

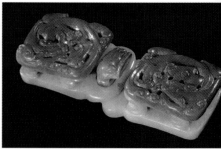

By the early nineteenth century, China's imperial court consumed most of Burma's jadeite output. Its intense colors immediately destined it for jewelry. Today such brilliant green jadeite would be cabbed for rings instead of carved for bangles (opposite). Once Burma's supplies increased, more jadeite carvings appeared, like the Qing Dynasty belt buckle (above), which incorporates the material's oxidized red skin as a design feature, or the justifiably famous two-tone cabbage (left), with two carved grasshoppers camouflaged on its leaves.

The last three forms, the *hu*, *huang*, and *chang*, are less known but still vital to all solemn rites because they, with the *kuei*, represented the four seasons and the four cardinal directions. The Chinese usually carved the *hu*, symbolic of Autumn and the West, in white jade, often incorporating a tiger. A *pi* cut in half is a *huang*, a semicircular representation of Winter, or the North, usually in black nephrite. Finally, halving a *kuei* leaves a *chang*. Typically carved of reddish jade, the *chang* symbolized Summer, or the South.

Before the emperor began a service with those six ceremonial or ritual jades, he walked toward the altar, his steps accented by the synchronous tinkling of twelve jade pendants adorning his robes. Worn only by the emperor, the dozen jades represented the twelve annual lunar cycles and the twelve hours of the Chinese day. When the emperor stood before him, the Chief of the Jade Storehouse opened the sealed box holding an empire's treasures—gems, gold, ivory, and the most precious of all objects, the ritual jades. The emperor took the *kuei*, the symbol of imperial power, in his right hand. Without it, even he could not approach the altar. In his left hand the emperor held the *pi*, the symbol of Heaven. Then, and only then, once he had grasped the ritual jades, did the emperor begin the service.

Despite the multimillennial relationship with nephrite, in 1784 A.D., quite late as Chinese history is calculated, an event of such magnitude occurred that the gem world still reels from its consequences. Among the cargoes that arrived in Beijing after a new trade agreement with Burma lay a material that turned the core, indeed the very heart, of Chinese civilization inside out. To this day it has not recovered. Once released, the brilliant temptress seduced an empire to abandon its past, luring it from its primal love with the folly of youth.

The seductress was jadeite, in vibrant colors that captivated a court and then its people. It dazzled China with its reds, yellows, whites, and jade greens the likes of which no one had seen before. Burmese jadeite was everything nephrite was not. It was bright, shiny, even gaudy, a new stone for a new age. It remains the proverbial tail wagging the dog. The typical young cutter in China, the new upwardly-mobile Chinese consumer, the *nouveau-riche* Hong Kong gem dealer, and particularly the overseas Chinese, and American jade buyers—almost all believe that jadeite alone has value. By reducing nephrite to a souvenir-carving material, how tragically far from its illustrious past the world has let slip the Stone of Heaven.

Jadeite is without doubt a wonderful gem and carving material. Because it has all three requirements for gem status—beauty, rarity, durability—it was destined to be enjoyed in jewelry. Even though other countries admire lavender jadeite, the second most valuable color, China prefers green. When its clarity, color, and luminescence attain the standard of imperial jade, its green rivals, many claim exceeds, the brilliance of emeralds.

Instantly jade was not just for rituals and religion. Practically overnight it became China's court favorite, a jade to wear, to show, to flaunt. While jadeite's popularity in jewelry cascaded through Chinese society, nephrite retained its place as the ritual Stone of Heaven. Gradually the Chinese substituted jadeite for nephrite in new ritual objects until finally, with a civil war and the rise of communism, they dropped the ritual use of jade altogether. More than a tinge of irony attends the capitulation of an egocentric insular culture like China's to an imported product from what it considered an insignificant neighbor worthy only of paying tribute. But capitulate it did, reserving the best, most beautiful green Burma jadeite for imperial and court use, much as white nephrite for millennia had been the perquisite of the court and the scholars.

Burmese jadeite's arrival in the late 1700s transformed China's use and concept of jade. No longer was white nephrite unique as the Stone of Heaven. Bright green jadeite articles, such as the belt dangle (right) and the praying mantis (opposite) captivated a new regal generation. Today most Asians and virtually all Westerners view jadeite as the jade of great value, completely reversing China's grand nephrite history.

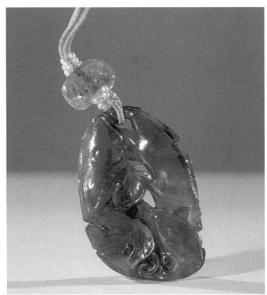

National Palace Museum, Taipei

Yü, the Chinese word for jade. Picture three pierced pieces of jade threaded onto a vertical string. Subtract the small dot or line on the bottom right to get the symbol meaning "one who rules." Represented by a pictograph believed to have originated in 2950 B.C., jade and ruler, both intermediaries between Heaven and Earth, share a single sign of power.

The Chinese never specifically limited the word *yü* to nephrite, the stone they most honored; once it meant "a precious stone of great beauty." Translators tell me *yü* now means "any hard, precious stone of great beauty." As appealing as the second definition sounds, it opens the door to considerable abuse. Although the Chinese had no jadeite when the word and symbol originated, today they use *yü* to refer to nephrite or jadeite. Often Chinese add "old" or "soft" to *yü* when referring to nephrite and "new" or "hard" when they mean jadeite. For most buyers, such nuances and the use of nonspecific adjectives further confuse an issue sorely in need of clarity.

As Burma's jadeite supplies increased in the 1800s, carvings appeared. Soon jadeite animals, objects, and gems outshone nephrite. For the past two hundred years (and disregarding the 5,000 years that preceded them) jadeite has been the preeminent stone and gem within China. It seems that no one objected to the culture's central substance being supplanted by a totally different material. Perhaps calling both *yü* eased the transition. Although some nephrite carving continued until the end of the Qing Dynasty, jadeite gained popularity and importance up to the 1911 revolution, which threw China into a lingering chaos that brought about Japan's conquest in the 1930s, the end of imperial China, and the overthrow by Mao's communists in 1948. In hundreds of interviews inside and outside China and dozens of books, I have never encountered any reluctance at any level of society to converting from nephrite to jadeite.

Initially the jadeite jewelry and carvings mimicked originals in

The Baur Collection, Geneva

nephrite, but with its unique qualities, the ingénue deserved a role of its own. Soon a jadeite style appeared, which is basically unchanged today. Burma jadeite, whether carved inside China, in Hong Kong, or in another of Asia's factories, typically is seen as simple cabochons for rings, earrings, or pins, bangles (most often undecorated), or carved pieces for pendants (usually angels, stylized mountains, or clouds).

Jadeite's green is unrivaled; the presence of Guatemala's jadeite (in use by the Olmec, Maya, and Aztecs in Mesoamerica for three thousand years) went unacknowledged in China. And the additional lavender color, as well as multiple hues within a single piece, inspired China's carvers to experiment with new styles. Objects that would have looked subdued in nephrite, such as the horse on page 21, the cabbage on page 22, the bangles on page 23, or the praying mantis above, became electric in jadeite. Prices reflect appeal and demand. Each year at gem shows such as Tucson or at large auctions in Hong Kong, some individual Burmese imperial Jade cabochons and pendants fetch more than $100,000. For a 10- to 15-carat piece much of the world views as a rock, that is a staggering price.

With their devotion to this gorgeous upstart, no price seems too great for buyers who both love jade and want to emulate the last of China's emperors by wearing imperial green. Now the cost of rough Burmese jadeite with desirable colors almost precludes its use for carving unless a specific shape has been commissioned by a buyer willing to pay gem prices for an object. China usually carves commercial-grade jadeite, which means mainly grays or muted colors. To produce the greatest financial return, intense colors are reserved for gems, leaving us with far fewer and less interesting carvings. The fabulous colors in jadeite carvings pictured throughout this book were possible only when emperors directed stone use. Fortunately, museums and collections have preserved the best for us to see.

THE OLMEC, MAYA, & AZTECS IN MESOAMERICA

Hernán Cortés led a ragtag band of Spanish soldiers from Cuba to Mexico in 1519. First the red-haired *conquistador* burned his ships to insure his unreliable "army" couldn't desert. Next he headed inland, toward the Aztec capital of Tenochtitlan—now Mexico City—aiming to conquer Emperor Moctezuma and his empire. Audaciously, with more gall than sense, a few hundred Spaniards confronted the city of 300,000 whose myths predicted the arrival of a red-haired god from afar. So they greeted Cortés with some warmth. Feigning friendship, Cortés captured Moctezuma, thus beginning Spanish domination that enslaved the people, plundered the land, and almost eradicated the indigenous culture. When the Aztecs grew alarmed at Spanish greed and passion for gold and silver, Moctezuma is said to have observed to his court, "Thank heaven they do not know about the *chalchihuites* (jades)."

Therein lies another tale of cultural clash. Nephrite that the Chinese loved beyond measure, most Europeans and Americans cast aside as only souvenir-carving material. Jadeite that the Aztecs, and the Maya before them, and the Olmec before them, honored as the most precious objects on earth, the Spanish *conquistadores* dismissed as green rocks.

Seeking a conciliatory gesture to avert pending conflict, Moctezuma told Cortés he wanted to give him some very valuable stones as a present for his king. Moctezuma supposedly said, "These are *chalchihuites*, not to be given to anyone but your king. Each is worth two loads of gold." Cortés was not impressed, but he did at least send them toward Spain. Unfortunately the jades never arrived. French pirates hijacked the three treasure ships carrying them and precious metals. But the Aztec sense of value survives. Moctezuma

Occasionally jade carvings transcend a single time or culture. This portrait pectoral, from the Olmec Preclassic period (1000-600 B.C.), was later honored by the Maya and most likely worn by a Mayan ruler.

The British Museum, London

27

had sent a message much like Confucius: gold has a value; jade is priceless.

After Cortés placed Moctezuma under elegant but strict house arrest, the two continued daily discussions, even playing a native chess-like game, ending it with a gift exchange. One day the Aztec king presented Cortés with large gold and silver disks, which obviously pleased the Spaniard. Noting this, in a desperate attempt to curry favor with the unenlightened infidels, Moctezuma promised that on the following day he would give the most precious gift of all. He offered Cortés three perfect jadeite beads, but, coveting gold and not beads, the *conquistador* was "bitterly disappointed."

Three grand conjectures attempt to explain how Mesoamericans came to work jade. I consider one to be outlandish, one farfetched, and one tantalizing. Most detached from the truth are writers who propose that the long, straight "runways" on Peru's high plains are alien landing strips and that jade knowledge came from space. In his popular book *Kon-Tiki*, Thor Heyerdahl postulates that boat people from Polynesia settled South America. If so, the theory goes, they could have brought jade skills gained from other islands. Even had the South American immigrants been Polynesians—which they were not—there is no evidence to show Polynesians who might have settled came from islands with jade skills.

Museum of Mankind, London (2)

Early Olmec jade mastery, as exhibited in these two masks, set a standard of excellence never exceeded in Middle America.

Mesoamerica's and China's historic and cultural relationships with jade did coincide, resulting in tantalizing parallels too great to ignore. Were they accidental? Did a relationship exist? Some scholars wonder if the famous "land bridge" that twice allowed people to migrate by foot from Siberia to Alaska (and then to disperse throughout the Americas) also transported Chinese skill with and devotion to jade. The 25,000 B.C. and 12,000 B.C. migration periods occurred long before any known Chinese association with jade. That said, I find striking similarities between Chinese jade history and what transpired in Mesoamerica.

Begin by comparing the Chinese figure on page 11 and the Costa Rican ax gods on pages 34-35. Also consider that the Maya (and sometimes the Aztecs) assembled burial jades even more elaborate than China's. Mesoamericans entombed royal personages wearing jade suits (similar to the Chinese suit on page 12) and masks, lying inside giant stone sarcophagi covered with jade. They arrayed their deceased in jade head bands, jade tubes to hold their hair in place, jade wrist cuffs, jade necklaces, ten jade rings, and surrounded them with personal jade objects. And ponder these other coincidences between China and Mesoamerica. The Aztecs named their brilliant green jadeite *quetzalitztli*, after their vibrantly-hued bird, the quetzal; in China the best green Burmese jadeite became *fei-ts'ui*, after the kingfisher's colorful feathers. And both the Maya and the Chinese shared beliefs of jade's extraordinary powers to heal the sick or injured, exorcise demons, prevent or delay body composition, and even bestow immortality.

The natives who had already populated the areas of and between what are now Mexico and Peru discovered jadeite and, on their own, mastered carving without the benefit of metals. The Olmec, who created the first culture in the Western Hemisphere, flourished on Mexico's Gulf Coast between 1300 B.C. and 400 A.D. Jade masters for more than a thousand years—during the same period when China's Shang and Zhou Dynasties produced elegant nephrite *pi*, *kuei*, and *ts'ung* symbols—the Olmec carved

unsurpassed human figures. Theirs are the strongest representations of human faces ever carved in jade. Although less well known, the Olmec brought jade carving to a level that allowed the Maya and Aztecs to build on a solid artistic and technical base.

After the rapacious Spanish assault on native culture and religion, Indians withdrew so far from their roots that subsequent generations not only did not know how to carve jade but had no idea even where to find it. Because Mesoamerican jade carvings older than the Olmec do not exist, we assume the Olmec first discovered New World jadeite. The mine or mines were lost to the world from the 1500s until the 1960s. As a result of some scientific sleuthing after World War II by William Foshag, Smithsonian's curator of geology, and archeologists in the 1960s (as well as a lucky jadeite find in 1957 by an American businessman), the search for the source of Mesoamerican jadeite not only centered on Guatemala but on a single location, the Motagua Valley. The dogged determination of an American couple, Mary Lou and Jay Ridinger, led them to discover *in situ* jadeite boulders. More exploration in the valley produced jadeite in a variety of colors and even old Mayan work sites where small outdoor carving factories had operated in fixed locations for centuries. Today's miners still find small pieces of worked and unworked jadeite, as well as tools and pottery.

Resolving another mystery, the source of foamy blue-green jadeite favored by Olmec carvers and often found in Costa Rican graves (see pages 34-35), a decade ago the Ridingers discovered the first such *in situ* boulder, thus proving that both the Olmec and Maya mined jade in the Motagua

Museum of Jade, San Jose, Costa Rica

Masters of the human form, Olmec and Maya jade carvers created remarkably durable records of their cultures. The strong figure with traditional features (opposite) dates from the Olmec Preclassic period, 1000-600 B.C. A unique flat tablet Olmec portrait (above), found on Costa Rica's Atlantic coast, appears to be topped with a crown. And the famous bas-relief Maya jade plaque dated 600-800 A.D. (below), uncovered at Teotihuacan, depicts an enthroned, regally dressed king accompanied by a court dwarf.

The British Museum, London

Cleveland Museum of Art, Cleveland

The mouths have it. A silent 1500s Aztec rabbit nestles an eagle warrior between its protective legs. The rabbit, the eagle warrior, and pulque beer were all born on the same day in the Aztec story of creation.

Agape in anger or terror? We will never know. Mosaic jade masks, such as this dramatic Zapotec interpretation (right), appeared over the more than three thousand years that several cultures flourished throughout Mesoamerica.

Rich Maya so treasured jade that they endured primitive inlays to make a fashion statement. Notice the beauty-notching of two of these teeth.

Dumbarton Oaks Research Library and Collections, Washington, D.C.

Dr. Guillermo Mata Collection

Valley. Their next quest was to locate the source of brilliant green jadeite that researchers had found in tombs all over Central America, particularly in El Salvador and Belize. No such color had appeared after years of mining in the Motagua Valley. The absence of emerald-green or imperial-green jadeite led to speculation that the Olmec had exhausted the original source or that another yet undiscovered mine held the secret. Then in the 1980s the Ridingers found a few boulders with small bright green spots—but without imperial jadeite's translucency—leading them to believe that the most desirable of all Mesoamerican jadeite colors originated in Guatemala's Motagua Valley, although never in large quantities.

Finally, we understand why the Olmec and Maya produced so many beautiful jadeite carvings whereas the Aztecs, even though they revered jade as much, made relatively few. Records indicate that the first two cultures had direct access to Guatemala's mining area; the Aztecs apparently had to rely on southern tribes, who paid tribute in jade, but kept their source secret. Based on jadeite colors and textures, we now believe that Guatemala's Motagua Valley supplied all or most of the jade used throughout Mesoamerica for

Mexican National Museum of Anthropology, Mexico City

about 3,000 years. To date no one has found another mine.

No one knows with certainty whether the Olmec and Mayan cultures blended into one around 300-400 A.D. or if the Maya developed separately farther north in Mexico. Either way, between 300-600 A.D. the Maya dominated Mesoamerica with one of the world's most advanced cultures. Their abstract reasoning, mathematical skills, 365-day calendar, sculptures, hieroglyphic writing, and architecture had no equal in feudal Europe. By the Late Classic Period, 600-900 A.D., an estimated fourteen million Maya lived in what are often described as the world's most modern urban centers of the time. And like the Chinese, although they had crystal gemstones, gold, and silver, the Maya made jade the focal point of their rituals, elevating it to the most important and precious material in their society. They also had what are for us some unpleasant ceremonial customs.

Jade knives and bowls played central ritual roles in human sacrifices and bloodletting, which the Maya commonly practiced in multiples at important events. Contrary to their unwarranted reputation as placid natives, the Maya sought conflict as a means to capture prisoners. And in the

33

All ax-gods from Museum of Jade, San Jose, Costa Rica except: #5 and #7, Frederick Mayer Collection and #8, Herman Paez Collection

Ax-gods, pendants with small figures atop stylized ax blades, are the most prevalent pre-Columbian jade artifacts found in Costa Rica. Although it is assumed the jadeite came from far north in Guatemala, it is unclear whether the ax-gods were carved in Costa Rica or brought there uncut or in other forms and fashioned locally. What is clear is that over centuries ax-god styles changed, beginning with a striking similarity to ancient Chinese carvings (above, far left) and ending with figures that support alien visitor theories (opposite, far right, and below).

civilization that followed, the ferocious and brutal Aztecs expanded sacrificial offerings to such an extent that they had difficulty maintaining an inventory of victims to keep up with ritual demands.

In Mesoamerica many substances carry "jade" or "jadeite" labels. The world contains numerous green and black stones. With no nephrite in Central America, anything marked *jade* should be jadeite, and certainly anything marked *jadeite* ought to be, because it is the proper name for a specific substance. Geologists, gemologists, and appraisers subscribe to this practice. But far too many archaeologists, museum curators, historians, grave robbers, and unscrupulous sellers prefer to lump anything the Olmec, Maya, and Aztecs carved under one convenient term, *jade*. This creates confusion that needs not be so, if not outright misrepresentation.

Kings were invariably buried with true jadeite, which proves that the original carvers knew the difference between jadeite and other stones, mainly by hardness and appearance. But workers cut the stones they had, and many of today's museum pieces contain mixtures of jadeite, diopside, albite, and numerous other materials. Only when a piece is composed of almost all jadeite, usually ninety percent or more, do gemologists label it *jade*. Other substances, like serpentine or chloromelanite, should be accurately identified. At least they should not be misidentified as jadeite. Academics recently have taken a strange stand, creating totally new terms like "cultural jade" and "social jade" to describe non-jadeite pre-Columbian carvings. The buying public needs to take notice of this dangerous practice.

THE MAORI IN NEW ZEALAND

D awn neared on the cold waters. Chilled passengers huddled to-gether in long canoes, surely wondering whether this would be the day they died, or the day they found land. With only a vague idea of the place from which they started, no idea where they were, and no way to know where they were going, the crew of men, women, and children paddled south by the stars, waiting for light, watching for a shore.

A thousand years have passed since the day the Maori arrived in New Zealand. By their language, culture, features, and legends, we know they were Polynesians, but precious little else. Their ancestors had migrated about 4,000 years ago from Southeast Asia across islands to the south and east. Some offspring island-hopped across much of the South Pacific, ultimately to the Marquesas Islands. From the south a group moved northward to inhabit the Hawaiian Islands, then south again to Tahiti. More than a thousand years passed until about 1000 A.D., when pressures built to make them travel once again. They took to canoes, finding their way across the trackless and dangerous Pacific to the Cook Islands and New Zealand. With them they carried yams, taro, and other tropical fruits and vegetables from their home islands. Instead of another warm paradise, they found a temperate rain forest, and on the South Island, glaciers, the Southern Alps, snow, ice, sleet, and for the first time in their lives, four distinct seasons. Their landfall provided a hidden blessing of monumental proportions. For on the beaches and in the streambeds along a large section of the island's western coast, the Maori found nephrite jade, a treasure the voyagers quickly mastered and which became, as museum director Russell Beck says, "the basis of the Maori way of life."

The significance of jade may be lost on today's readers. Remember, when they arrived in New Zealand, the Maori were neolithic, or Stone Age, people, and they remained so until first Abel Tasman (in 1642) "discovered" and then Captain James Cook (in 1769) "rediscovered" them and their

The **tiki** *figurine, virtually the symbol of New Zealand's Maori, is best known of all their carved jade shapes. The Maori call the amulet* **hei-tiki**. **Hei** *means "to tie around the neck" and* **tiki**, *"human," "ancestor," or "the first person."*

Museum of New Zealand, *Te Papa Tongarewa*, Wellington

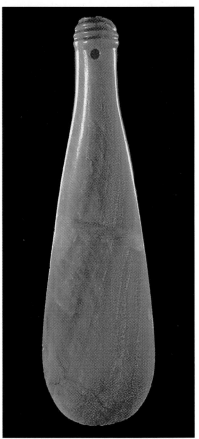

For the British and Americans, a mace is the symbol of power and authority. For New Zealand's Maori, natives of Polynesian heritage, a short (app. 16 inches or 40 cm) bat carved from local nephrite served the purpose. The mere *(pronounced meer-ree), originally used as a war club and jabbing weapon, evolved to symbolic duty. Often carved from a specific variety of New Zealand nephrite called* Inanga, *a* mere *hung from the wrist via a plaited flax cord threaded through a drill hole. This example, probably in use before Captain Cook arrived in 1769, displays all the desirable characteristics of the symbolic nephrite tool— rarity, beauty, and toughness.*

The Topi family, Ruapuke Island, New Zealand

islands. Before the Europeans arrived, the Maori had never seen metal. Aside from food and shelter, as Beck told me, "jade provided the Maori with tools, weapons, ceremonial objects, and personal ornaments, the only stone in the world that could have served all those needs."

Nephrite jade most likely enabled the Maori to survive in New Zealand. Harder and tougher than any metal the British later brought, nephrite did for the Maori what jade had already done for the Swiss stilt-house culture, the ancient Chinese, and the Olmec and Maya. With jade, the Maori possessed Stone Age tools and weapons with metal-like properties. Blades of jade hold sharp edges better than iron. Adzes and axes performed double duty for woodworking and fighting. Clubs, called *mere*, the Maori perfected for hunting seals and moa, New Zealand's now-extinct flightless bird, and for battles. Though they were a relatively small group with common ancestry who arrived in several migratory waves, presumably from the same original home, the Maori did battle with each other. Unlike most Native Americans who did not conceive of owning even a part of the earth, the Maori developed a system of land ownership. Disputes over land and personal property provided suitable cause for frequent armed conflicts. And because it was hard, heavy, and tough, warriors armed themselves with jade.

By the 12th century, jade work areas dotted several beaches on the South Island's west coast. Another 200 years saw jade use expand to become a fundamental part of Maori life. Some people specialized in collecting jade, others in carving. Because the North Island had no jade source, the South Islanders developed a jade trade. As did the Chinese and Maya, soon the Maori expanded tool- and weapon-making to include art, ornaments, and ritual objects. But the Maori remained in the Stone Age until Europeans arrived. Thus, their jade applications reflect the scope of their society. Basically they used jade as tools and weapons, and decorated both. Although they never achieved a written language, the Maori sense of design and workmanship surpassed other Polynesian groups. In the absence of contact with any other people, the Maori developed their own culture with jade, utilizing its properties of light, translucency, sound, color, and feel. They even altered colors and hardness by heating. The Maori's unique style shows their reverence and appreciation for the material.

A chronicle of the *tiki*, by far the best known of all Maori ornaments, explains much of recent Maori jade history. Most likely of Polynesian origin in wood or bone, the figures are properly called *hei-tiki*, which means "human pendant". They show a large-headed human figure, either a male or a female, squatting with heels together and hands on thighs. The tilted head measures about half the height of the figure. The Maori refined the figure and defined its ultimate shape and style in jade.

But it appears the Maori had relatively few *tiki* carvings when Captain Cook arrived. Like foreign tourists today, the English crews wanted souvenirs, and the Maori complied, making so many to trade for British metal objects that they ran low on jade. Russell Beck says that even after they started carving their jade adzes into figures, they still could not supply the demand. So several European families in Dunedin went into the *tiki* business, wholesaling their own non-Maori carvings to Maoris on the North Island for reselling, retailing to other New Zealand Europeans, and exporting to overseas traders. As you might expect, various museums around the world display these European-carved *tiki* as original Maori art.

By the end of the 1800s, local Maori, dominated by British culture, no longer wanted to carve jade. But they had already created a global demand for the one souvenir from New Zealand every visitor seemed to want. A hemisphere away, the world's leading stone-carving town, Germany's Idar-Oberstein, filled the void. Between 1896 and 1914, four Idar families sold more than a million *tiki* figures carved in Germany, far more than all the Maori had ever made in their thousand-year history. Hubert Dalheimer, whose grandfather imported enough New Zealand nephrite before World War I to last the firm until the 1930s, told me his father said, "We never could understand where all the figures were going, and then we started seeing our own work showing up in European museums, labeled 'Maori *tiki* carving.'"

Curators are not the only ones confused. Although the Maori named all aspects of jade, including its various colors, its sources, and the objects they carved, in New Zealand practically no one calls jade by either of its names, *nephrite* or *jade*. New Zealanders created a unique word, *greenstone*, to refer

not only to nephrite but also to bowenite, a translucent serpentine found near Milford Sound as well as in China. That colloquial term frustrates the market, sellers and customers alike, who differentiate prices and investments by the material they are trading. The Maori dismiss buyer frustration, saying it is a silly problem for *Pakeha*, meaning "any New Zealander who isn't native." They themselves prefer using *Pounamu*. In reality, the native term maintains the confusion because the Maori also call both local nephrite and bowenite *Pounamu*. So much for clarity.

The Maori, like so many other native cultures, recently began rediscovering their past. Just as natives press land issues in Canadian and U.S. courts and legislatures, so too do the Maori seek redress from New Zealand for the land and culture they feel they lost. Maori activism affects jade. Even though their ancestors all but abandoned jade carving last century and only a few Maori now express themselves in the medium, they want to control most jade areas, lock out local non-native miners when their leases expire, and tie up much of the raw material. Their activism and restrictions are creating a jade shortage, forcing non-native New Zealand carvers, who prefer working in local material, to import British Columbian nephrite instead.

Representing less than ten percent of New Zealand's three-and-a-half million people, the Maori won back rights to the South Island's main jade conduit, the Arahura River, from source to sea. The name *Arahura*, has significance for the Maori. It describes a star path to guide them at sea, the

Today's world-class New Zealand carving is done mainly by a small group of non-Maori Kiwis. Donn Salt has a global following for his masterful work (above). Most of the world's jade tiki *were carved between 1896 and 1914 by German craftsmen in Idar-Oberstein. More than a million went back to New Zealand for sale. Idar's Dieter Jerusalem (right) holds a tray of New Zealand jade carved by his great-uncles. Hubert Dalheimer (opposite, top) keeps his grandfather's tradition alive by filling new orders for old* tiki.

path to the west. Sure enough, the Arahura River flows westward from the jade mountains to the ocean on New Zealand's south island. Of relevance to anthropologists, the name *Arahura* is also used in both Tahiti and the Cook Islands.

Until the last two decades, New Zealand saw very little jade-carving activity and even less Maori involvement. But both are changing rapidly now. Whereas once only souvenir shops worked with local nephrite, almost simultaneously several European-heritage carvers emerged on both New Zealand's islands, transforming the quality, style, artistic content, and public recognition of Kiwi carving. Maori legal activity has also raised native awareness, inspiring a new generation of native carvers. Most successful of these young artists is Hepi Maxwell (below).

With the legacy of Maori jades, New Zealanders, using local nephrite whenever possible to sell domestically and internationally, have leapt to the forefront of the world's jade carvers. Breaking all barriers that had tied nephrite and jadeite carving to styles from the past—China, Maya, Maori, and Russia's Fabergé, this revolutionary Kiwi band (see pages 54-55) are redrawing the image of jade carving today.

Hepi Maxwell (left) is the best of a new generation of Maori jade carvers (see page 54). One favorable outcome of a continuing land-rights struggle between natives and the New Zealand government may be renewed Maori interest in carving local nephrite, which both non-native New Zealanders and Maori call "greenstone."

JADE TODAY

Two stories illustrate the state of jade today, one economic and one spiritual. A Chinese gentleman stood smiling behind the Hong Kong store counter, never wavering in his assumption of the truth. I had asked to see his best jade, and he produced a Burmese jadeite ring. I refined my query, asking to see nephrite carvings. "But," he said, "this is *real* jade." "So is nephrite," I replied. "Oh," he said, "are you looking for *soft* jade?" "No," I repeated, "I want to see nephrite." "Oh," he said again, "you want *old* jade." "No," I said for the third time, "I do not care if the carvings are old or new. I just want to see your best." "Then you want to see *precious* jade, our jadeite from Burma."

In Thailand Phra Yanaviriyajan awoke with a vision. In it he learned he must make the world's largest jade Buddha. The monk flew to Burma, viewed jadeite, and declared it did not fulfill his vision. He returned, waited, and prayed. Then he read about Canada's jade. He asked disciples there to find his boulder, but they could not. After two years he had another vision. When he called the disciples to say his boulder was now in Canada, they said they had nothing yet. Yes, he said, it was already there and he intended to fly to Canada immediately. That very morning the Vancouver *Sun* featured miner Kirk Makepeace standing by his new find, a massive nephrite boulder. Having arrived, the monk went directly to the boulder, felt it, and declared his vision realized; this was his Buddha. Today the statue rests in its own temple (see page 57). From the collected scraps and dust, the monk made 500,000 tiny Buddha carvings, which the devout bought.

I see two markets —jewelry and carving—for both jades, with wide price variations. Burma's imperial-green jadeite dominates jade jewelry. No other contemporary jade can command more than $100,000 per piece. By comparison, Guatemala green, white, and black jadeite jewelry seldom surpasses $1,000-2,000. Both countries produce carving material, more subdued and in less desirable colors, but jewelry drives the jadeite market.

With nephrite, jewelry and carving prices are very different. Nephrite jewelry is usually inexpensive, often relegated to souvenir products. But following in China's great carving tradition, most fine jade art today is in nephrite, done in New Zealand and Canada. More carvings are made, usually as novelties, almost all at much lower prices than in jadeite.

In 1968 an elephant carried a Hong Kong buyer to northern Burma's jadeite source. Hoarding his rare treasure, the shop owner sold this five-carat Imperial-green jadeite ring in 1986 for $33,000. I have been offered $200,000 to find its duplicate, a task that has proved impossible.

Burma's Jadeite

Most of Burma's jadeite—and its rubies, sapphires, teak, and heroin—reaches the outside world through smuggling. If given a choice, smuggling small, light gemstones makes much more sense than smuggling trees and boulders. But Burmese jadeite is no ordinary rock, and such great profits await anyone successfully negotiating a human or animal mule trail from northern Burma to either Thailand or China that the black-market game engages many players. Whether carried out illegally or sold at the biannual government emporium in Rangoon (below), almost all Burma's jadeite ends up in China or Hong Kong for cutting.

The ultimate Chinese gem gamble is buying jadeite boulders. They are sold either sliced or with a small "window" polished to whet buyers' appetites. I have seen boulders sell at auction in Rangoon (and illegally in Chiang Mai, Thailand) for over a million dollars apiece, with no more than an inch of green peeking through one corner. What lies beyond is anyone's guess. Green spots within boulders are cut into gems; large areas without marketable jewel colors become carvings. As many buyers lose as win.

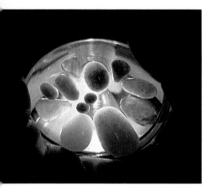

Burma's military government controls official buying channels, but smuggling remains the dealers' route of choice to enter Thai and Chinese markets. In clandestine venues throughout Burma, sellers display black-market jadeite atop flashlights (above), at night or in back rooms. At the annual Gems, Jade, and Pearls Emporium in Rangoon, a silent auction that brings more than $11 million, the government offers about 500 lots of rough jadeite (right) mainly to Chinese bidders.

Hing Wa Lee Jewelers, Inc.

Courtesy of John Ng

Burmese jadeite cabochons and carvings set as jewelry, dark green up to and including imperial-green, are today's most expensive jades. Depth of color, intensity, clarity, and translucency all affect price. More plentiful pale shades cost less, including the popular apple-green. When jadeite achieves a deep, vibrant lavender, prices soar, often reaching several hundred thousand dollars for a matched set (above). Burma's jadeite comes in a variety of colors, including yellow, orange, red, white, cream, and black, but high-ticket jewelry concentrates on only green and lavender. Well done carvings with spots of good color also fetch big prices.

Seldom does a gem material have only one source and one market, but at the pinnacle of jadeite pricing, only Burma jade is considered by the trade to be a gem, and almost exclusively Asians buy such quality. Rarity skyrockets prices, and Burma's top green and lavender jadeite qualify as some of the rarest gems known. Demand for large, fine material follows Asia's economic upswings; successful businessmen spend big money on themselves and the women in their lives. Burma jadeite stands without competition as the most desirable gemstone in Asia, especially for people of Chinese heritage no matter where they live.

Ominously, more imperial-green Burmese jadeite is sold than mined. When people willingly pay hundreds of thousands of dollars for genuine Burmese imperial jadeite, then beware of counterfeiters. Such success spawns imitations and fraud. Most common imitations are off-color, usually white or gray jadeite, dyed to bright green or lavender. Be on guard against carvings or cabochons of glass, agate, serpentine, chrysoprase, aventurine, calcite, amazonite, bowenite, soapstone, quartz, and dyed stones like quartzite, as well as plastic when falsely represented as jadeite.

45

China's Mining & Carving

Nephrite jade from China's far western border area is not actually mined—it is collected. In the Kunlun Mountains, each spring thaw rushes enough water into the White Jade and Black Jade Rivers to extract jade pebbles and boulders from the banks and sweep them downstream toward Hotan, a stop on the old Silk Road. Jade pickers (right), farmers with an eye good enough to separate jade from other rocks and a back strong enough to carry boulders downhill for days, can make a year's salary in a month or two. Once a week China's jade-buying office in Hotan holds a viewing (opposite), takes what it wants at a price it sets, and returns the remainder to the pickers, supposedly for their own use.

  Paradoxes abound concerning the source of white nephrite jade, the most valuable commodity in the empire throughout thousands of years of Chinese history. Both China and Taiwan insist that now-exhausted multiple mainland sources once supplied the realm. No proof confirms such sites. In fact, unlike gold mines, oil fields, or any number of other natural resources, I find evidence that every jade mine ever worked anywhere in the world is still producing jade. China's sole nephrite source, long kept secret by all parties, was and is more than 2000 miles from the imperial court in Beijing, in the Kunlun Mountains south of Hotan. Until it overran Turkestan in the 1950s, China only infrequently controlled this desert area outside its far western border. Today, Uygur tribesmen still pick up each boulder by hand, retrieving only a ton of white nephrite annually and 10-20 tons of green and black.

China cannot begin to supply its numerous jade industries with domestically-produced jade. But no other white nephrite has the historic significance of its Kunlun Mountains site or the character of its creamy appearance and texture. Russia's white nephrite sometimes appears chalky by comparison. South Korea's white nephrite is tinged with pale green. Crystal-line white jadeite from either Burma or Guatemala has a harder look and feel than Kunlun's subtle "oily" nephrite. China's emperors reserved white nephrite, the gorgeous material that has always been in short supply, for court use. But now, unlike in those periods when India bought nephrite directly from Hotan, only the Chinese government can legally buy Kunlun jade. To keep its factories busy, China also imports Burmese jadeite and British Columbian nephrite, and mines dozens of other cuttable rocks and minerals.

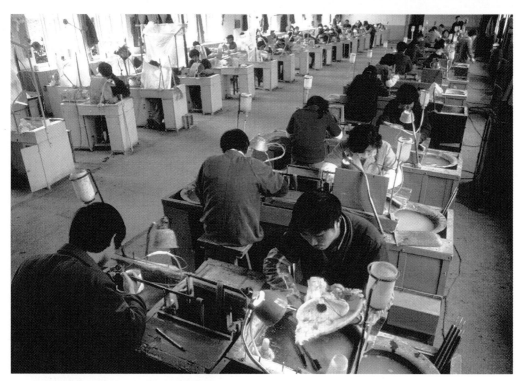

Of the 40 or so stone-carving factories in China, Yangzhou does most of the best jade work. Its 370 carvers use diamond-tipped electric drills to cut stone blocks marked by the factory's designer (left). This youthful, government-trained work force sculpt several large unique pieces a year, which breaks the monotony of repetitive contract work. Sadly, only a few independent artists carve in China.

China's 5,000-year-imperial history ended in 1911 with the downfall of its last powerful government. Between then and the conclusion of World War II, China's jade-carving tradition almost died. When Chairman Mao and his communist regime later opened a number of "jade-carving factories," it was not to rekindle the country's ancient heritage but to install foreign currency profit centers.

Few of the new factories carved any jade at all, and none carved only jade. Most worked with agate, quartz, soapstone, bowenite, serpentine, chrysoprase, and numerous other stones China either mined or imported. When the government did distribute jade for carving, it was usually jadeite from Burma, not nephrite from the Kunlun Mountains. Later, as sales increased, China contracted with British Columbia's Kirk Makepeace, the world's largest nephrite producer, for more than 200 tons of jade annually. But, disconnected from their own jade heritage, the Chinese rarely seek jade for artistic, symbolic, religious, or ritual objects. Disregarding their reverence in ages past, they relegate luxurious nephrite to inexpensive beads, jewelry, and souvenir carvings.

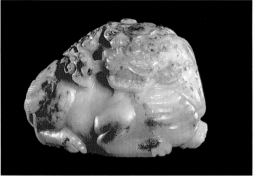

Fred Ward collection

As China develops its border areas, factories in distant Xinjiang Province (top, left), site of China's only jade source, teach teenagers to carve local nephrite. Even though the Yangzhou factory, on the east coast, has electricity and power tools (right), it maintains eight-foot treadles as a bridge to its cultural jade past so artists can produce several traditional pieces annually. A 43-year-old female carver spent four months hand-fashioning the above mythical beast from a White Jade River cobble.

This situation persists, the result of a socialist system where bureaucrats and entrepreneurs instead of emperors or artists make decisions. Young students with the best grades move upward through high schools and universities. Dropouts who fail the all-important regular school tests are assigned to factories, earning a dollar or two a day. Stone factories are like all others, receiving new workers from a pool of youths without the skills, intellect, or motivation to pass tests. Jade carving, most honored of all arts and crafts in ancient China, has fallen into the hands of underachievers for whom it is a job, not a passion. Without access to raw materials, tools, and a market, gifted carvers have little choice but to fill factory orders on assembly lines instead of taking artistic risks for creative satisfaction.

Remarkably, on a floor with a hundred other carvers, a few do excel, producing extraordinary work they do not own and cannot sell. They remain cogs in the greater China industrial wheel. At the moment, the grand, historic, and unsurpassed Chinese jade tradition fades. Revival cannot come under the present government system. Only the freedom to explore and create, to produce carvings as art, to love the material and respect it as history's special and unique stone will spark a change. But nothing will change as long as children with no knowledge of history remain only drills for hire.

49

Guatemala's Mayan Legacy

"Galactic Gold" cabochons and artifacts courtesy Jades, S.A., Antigua, Guatemala

An American couple, Mary Lou and Jay Ridinger, explore Guatemala's Motagua Valley and create new designs (right) from the historic material they mine there. Most authorities believe they have located the source of Mesoamerica's jadeite, lost to the world for centuries. While searching for bright green material, the Ridingers discovered a previously unknown rich opaque-black "Galactic Gold" jadeite, naturally embedded with various heavy metals (above).

Photos of mask above and necklaces opposite by Daniel Chauche

Jay Ridinger makes replicas of famous jade mosaic masks from jadeite boulders he mines in the Motagua Valley, the Mayan source.

As one of the three surviving jade cultures, Mesoamerica owes much of its current success with jadeite to Mary Lou and Jay Ridinger and sales to Guatemala's foreign visitors. Jades, S.A. mines its own jadeite and produces a full line of popular jewelry as well as replicas handmade by Mayan descendants from the jade treasured and revered by priests and rulers. To its credit, in a practice all too rare, Jades, S.A. clearly marks replicas as such.

Foreign domination by the English and Spanish severed native links to an historic jade past in New Zealand and Mesoamerica. In both areas non-native interest was initially responsible for an explosive growth in local carving. Now New Zealand and Canadian non-native carvers are generating renewed global awareness of jade designs as fine art. First-generation Guatemalan carvers are just beginning to realize the impact local jadeite had on their ancestors.

Canada's Jade Bounty

Tom Talpey, Shades of Jade

British Columbia's Kirk Makepeace (left) mines more jade than any other person or, for that matter, any country. Although China buys most, he ships rough nephrite to a score of other countries. Tom Talpey uses nephrite's stained-glass translucency to handcraft exquisite lampshades reminiscent of Tiffany's. He precisely cuts and fits each tile for his own masterpieces (above). In my business, Jade Designs, we slab boulders for the world's largest and finest one-piece jade tabletops and bookends.

Jade Designs

Debbie Wilson (3)

Besides producing most of the world's nephrite, Canada is also justly famous for its jade carvers. Unlike New Zealand, Canada's native Indian and Eskimo populations (who had access to jade historically) never moved beyond using the tough hard stones for tools. Only after British Columbia's vast deposits developed into a world-class resource did non-native artists begin art-carving nephrite.

Today, Canada's top jade carvers display a deep understanding of the material. Debbie Wilson, whose octopus, starfruit, and pepper appear here, began, as did others, by carving Canadian animals. Soon she and Lyle Sopel, another fine artist-carver, expanded their separate visions, growing as they saw jade's potential. Now they, like the old Chinese masters they emulate, work in concert with jade, their chosen medium of expression.

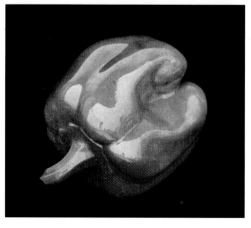

New Zealand's Innovative Jade Carvers

Hepi Maxwell (2)

Neil Hanna

New Zealand's artists produce some of the world's best contemporary jade carvings. Hepi Maxwell, the only Maori represented here, lives close to nature and relies on natural themes to link his Maori past to today's world. From one of nature's toughest, most difficult-to-carve materials, Ian Boustridge, a master of the medium, elicits delicate swirls suggesting tree ferns near his home. Neil Hanna combines black Australian nephrite with local jade in ceremonial fish hooks. Donn Salt works local nephrite with impeccable skill, coaxing from his imagination avant-garde pieces in great demand by tourists and local collectors.

Donn Salt

Ian Boustridge (2)

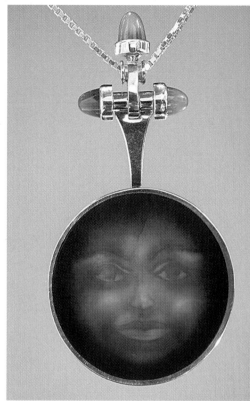

Donn Salt

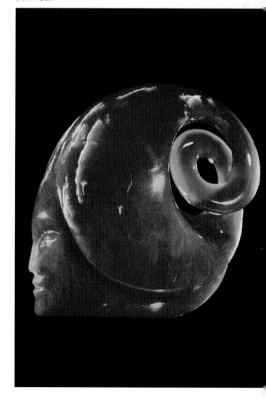

*New Zealand's new breed of jade carvers
stand alone in the world for their
individual carving styles and skills.
Almost all who enter the field as artists
are young and non-native. Having long
left animal and tiki figures that mire
others in mediocrity, the inspired carvers
expand jade design with impeccable
technique. Only the best of the Canadian
artists match the New Zealanders'
innovative forms and flawless finishes.
Unlike jade carvers in China, Hong
Kong, or Taiwan, who mainly repeat
traditional forms, New Zealand's
carvers are sculpting a new page in the
glorious history of nephrite jade.*

At the turn of this century the famous French jeweler Fabergé operated a studio in Moscow, which concocted some of the most fabulous objets d'art *in history. Most famous for his elaborate golden enameled eggs, Fabergé preferred incorporating Siberian nephrite into utility pieces for the royal family's daily use as well as spectacular state gifts, such as a cannon for Kaiser Wilhelm II.*

The principal commercial nephrite sites lie in British Columbia, Canada, which ships more than 300 tons annually. Besides Australia, New Zealand, and Russia, most countries have only minor occurrences. Burma and Russia supply most of the world's jewelry-grade jadeite in a variety of colors, and Guatemala mines black, gray, and green jadeite, often used for carvings and beads.

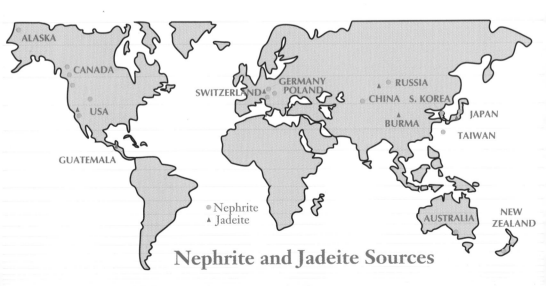

Nephrite and Jadeite Sources

At seven-tons, Thailand's first true "Jade Buddha" is also the world's largest (right), and could only have originated in British Columbia. The newest and most exciting jade discovery, Polar Jade, also from B.C., is the brightest, hardest nephrite ever found (bottom) and the first to color-compete with jadeite for jewelry. Australia produces the blackest of black nephrite (swan below). The most unusual jade mine is underwater. Sculptor Don Wobber (below, right) dives at Jade Cove, California, for nephrite washed from the cliffs. Floating ton-sized boulders with inner tubes, Wobber carves them into free-form pieces of ocean art or bathroom appointments.

Jade Designs

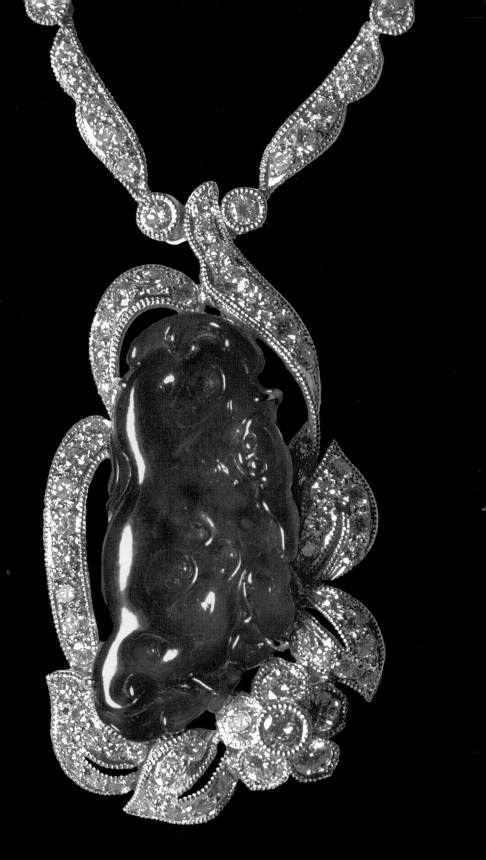

BUYING AND CARING

With most of my books, the last chapter is about equally divided between buying and caring. Such is not the case here. Caring for jade is relatively easy and will be covered briefly. But buying either nephrite or jadeite is more difficult than for almost any other gemstone. Confusion, deception, and fraud are deliberate with these stones, so we will carefully look at the joys of jade ownership as well as some precautions to make you more secure jade buyers.

For clarity, I will deal with jadeite first, then nephrite. With both I will cover buying old and new pieces, as jewelry and as carvings. What follows is what I have found to be a checklist for quality and value.

Jadeite artifacts exist mainly as carvings from both Mesoamerica and China and as jewelry from China. Occasionally a Mayan jewelry piece enters the market, but its sale generally is handled as if it were a carving. Despite what you may be told, it does make a difference that Mesoamerican relics be jadeite. Museums may display other materials equally, and archaeologists may admire albite carvings as much as jade, but when you buy, jadeite cost more, and it will be worth more should you resell. Mesoamericans understood stone differences, did their best carvings in jade, and reserved true jadeite for royal tombs. Insist on verification by a gemologist, appraiser, or a gem lab that the material in question is genuine, and have its age or period noted on the sales receipt. Make independent verification of the factual part of any purchase.

Technically there is no such thing as old Chinese jadeite carvings or jewelry, because the Burmese material was introduced only in 1784, late by Chinese standards. However, artifacts from then until the 1911 revolution are available. Unlike nephrite, used for symbols and ornaments, jadeite mainly went to jewelry and to carvings. For the buyer of these Chinese jadeites, the main concern should be authenticity. First, you must determine

Burma still produces small quantities of brilliant imperial-green jadeite, such as once captivated Chinese royalty. The material's high price destines it for use in jewelry. Fine jadeite typically becomes cabochons for rings or carvings, such as "Bat on Mountain," which, with 8 carats of diamonds in a platinum necklace, is priced at more than $200,000.

Hing Wa Lee Jewelers, Inc.

Nephrite spiral pendants by Ian Boustridge

Problems seldom arise with name artists, who proudly and accurately identify their jade. Not so in Hong Kong's outdoor jade market, where much of the green jadeite is dyed and many "old" pieces are new. Bargains occasionally appear, but buyers should be observant and cautious.

that the material is jadeite. Then you need to know if it is dyed, and lastly if it is new. Huge price leaps occur when jadeite jewelry and carvings possess anything approaching imperial-green color. Because the temptation is great to augment color, always suspect dyeing. Labs use spectroscopes to reveal dyes. You can learn to spot clumps of color and unusual concentrations of dye along tiny fractures. As a rule, question all brilliant green and lavender material, and put the proof on the seller.

Jade cannot be dated like dinosaur bones. Look for styles and carving techniques to suggest age. Before this century, jade was carved without electrical tools or diamond grit. Magnified examination shows smooth tiny lines and curves in genuine artifacts and sharp edges and corners on new pieces. One additional recent complication with China occurred when contemporary jewelry prices exceeded artifact value. The result has been to incorporate old jadeite pieces (either recut or "as is") into new jewelry, making it increasingly difficult to identify the jewelry or jade as *old* or *new*.

With new jadeite carvings or jewelry, watch out for dyeing. Dyeing jadeite is endemic. You may also occasionally find bleaching. And at least thirty other materials are sold as jadeite in China alone. To fool the unwary, sellers write receipts for soapstone, bowenite, serpentine, agate, quartz, and dozens of other stones, unscrupulously noting them as *yü* or *jade*.

Black nephrite cabochon earrings by Blue Planet Gems

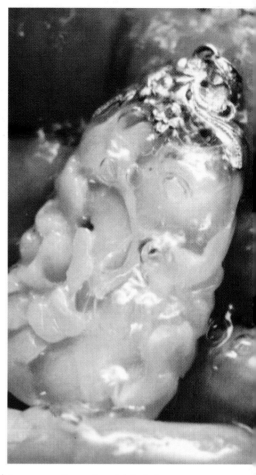

Fortunately, both nephrite (above) and jadeite (right), are among the most durable of gems. Both are considered safe for use in ultrasonic cleaners and both respond well to cleaning with soap and warm water. Both jades are harder than most steel; on the Mohs scale of 1-10 (with talc 1, gold 3, quartz 7, and diamond 10) jadeite is 6½-7 and nephrite is 6-6½. Jade will likely be one of the hardest components of your jewelry. Jade can scratch your gold, platinum, and silver; it is likely to be scratched only by harder crystal gemstones, diamonds, rubies, sapphires, and emeralds. For safety, store individual jewelry pieces in separate bags.

Nephrite is usually seen in great old Chinese carvings. As with jadeite, age is determined by style and surface detail. Finding comparative pieces is also easier with Chinese artifacts, and far more experienced appraisers and collectors are available to help. Nephrite is rarely encountered in ancient jewelry. Through the ages, the Chinese mainly carved nephrite objects, not gems.

Except for the creations of talented nephrite artists in Canada and New Zealand, most contemporary carving barely rises beyond souvenirs. For serious carvers, nephrite is a field awaiting rediscovery. But jewelry use grows yearly. Because nephrite is less costly, people today consume more nephrite jewelry than jadeite. Most of it goes into inexpensive beads and cabochons for rings and earrings. British Columbia supplies most of the green nephrite fashioned in China or Taiwan. The main scam by sellers is substitution, delivering agate, aventurine, dull chrysoprase, quartz, glass, and other green material and marking it as *nephrite* or *jade*.

Because both jadeite and nephrite are hard, durable, and resistant to most chemicals, caring for them is safe and simple. Wash with soap and water or use an ultrasonic cleaner as needed. Jade is likely to be the strongest part of any jewelry. Both jades are trouble-free companions, already tens of millions of years old, that will provide you with decades of pleasure and wear.

A Question of Value...

Because jadeite enjoys the premier position as the jade of choice for jewelry and investment, the chart (opposite) deals with jadeite, not nephrite. When a newly-cut imperial-green Burmese ring cabochon out-prices an authentic 3,000-year-old Chinese nephrite carving, the market has spoken. Once that is understood, then buying jadeite becomes a question of value. With jadeite, color and transparency determine price and value.

The chart is arranged principally for understanding Burma jadeite colors and learning how they are valued. Representative Guatemalan colors provide a comparison, and sample surface patterns demonstrate appearances other than those seen on ideal translucent cabochons.

Moving to the right across the top row steps toward perfection: the top right cab is imperial green. The color that experts agree is the rarest and most expensive is pure green. Any move away from that intense green results in diminished quality and lower prices.

Row two represents what the trade calls "apple green." It has good value, but not as high as imperial green. Darker tones are more valuable. After green, lavender is the second most-desired color, shown on row three. The deepest, richest lavenders command highest prices, whereas pale or bluish pieces sell for less. Burmese jadeite also comes in a variety of other colors. Those typically used for jewelry are red, orange, gold, and yellow. White and gray are common Burma colors, but most such material is sold for carvings.

Although Guatemala has produced brilliant green jadeite, its regular output consists of the hues shown—almost always heavily patterned, except for a smooth black jadeite that is popular for jewelry. On the world market, only the best colors of jadeite from either Burma or Guatemala bring a premium. All the rest sell as commercial carving stones.

As an unfaceted gem material either carved or cut into cabochons, jadeite relies on color and clarity for its look. Sold usually by the piece and not by the carat, jade is priced by appearance and impression. When it glows green as a newly-mown field at dawn and takes your breath away, it has value.

Jadeite Colors

Typical Burma Jadeite Colors

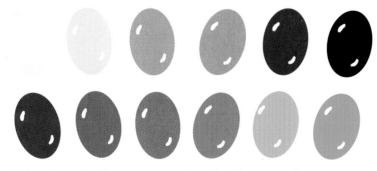

Typical Guatemala Jadeite Colors

Moss-in-Snow   Mottled   Rootlike   Variegated   Cracked   Mottled

Surface Characteristics and Patterns

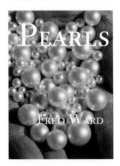

About Fred Ward and his Gem Book Series

Along the White Jade River in western China

Glamour, intrigue, romance, the quest for treasure... those are all vital aspects of humankind's eternal search and love for gemstones. As long as people have roamed the world, they have placed extraordinary value on our incredible gifts from the land and sea.

Jade is the sixth in a series of gem books written and photographed by Fred Ward. Each book, *Rubies & Sapphires, Emeralds, Diamonds, Pearls, Gem Care,* and *Jade,* is part of a 17-year global search into the history, geology, lore, and sources of these priceless treasures. He personally has visited the sites and artifacts displayed here to provide the most authentic and timely information available in the field. Fred Ward's original articles on these topics first appeared in *National Geographic* Magazine. In addition to being a journalist, Mr. Ward is a Graduate Gemologist (GIA), the highest academic achievement in the gem trade.

Mr. Ward, a respected authority on gems and gemology, is in great demand as a speaker to professional and private groups. After years viewing the global gem trade, he formed Blue Planet Gems, Inc. with designer Carol Tutera to make his vast experience available to others. He also owns Jade Designs, which distributes nephrite tabletops, bookends, and tombstones, as well as the brilliant new Polar Jade material.

For those interested in printing mechanics, this book is part of the ongoing computer desktop publishing revolution. It was designed entirely with PageMaker electronic layouts on a Mac Quadra 950. *Jade* was printed by H & D Graphics in Hialeah, Florida, using Adobe Janson typefaces.